**To
my dog,
Sam**

"If you don't own a dog, at least one, there is not necessarily anything wrong with you, but there may be something wrong with your life."

ROGER CARAS
A Celebration of Dogs

101

Things Dogs Do To Annoy Their Owners

RAY COMFORT

genesis
PUBLISHING GROUP

101 Things Dogs Do To Annoy Their Owners

Published by
Genesis Publishing Group
2002 Skyline Place
Bartlesville, OK 74006
www.genesis-group.net

Edited by Lynn Copeland

Illustrations by Richard Gunther,
www.mightymag.org

Cover, page design, and layout by Genesis Group

ISBN 978-1-933591-19-3

Printed in the United States of America

Introduction

I n September 2012, Florida resident Steve Gus-
tafson did something that brought tears to
my eyes. Steve and his dog, Bounce, were out
in their yard when Bounce was pounced on by a
hungry, seven-foot alligator and dragged into a
pond. Yelling, "You're not going to get her!" the
66-year-old grandfather did a belly flop on top of
the 130-pound alligator and managed to free his
beloved dog from the beast's jaws. They both es-
caped with minor injuries. What moved me was
what he said to a reporter who suggested that
what he did was a little dangerous. "What choice
did I have?" he asked. "That's my best friend. I didn't
think. You just react." Such is the power of love. If
you are a dog lover, you will understand.

Let me tell you about my dog, Sam.[1]

When our dog, Mandy, died, we decided that
we would live dog-less for a time. I'm the dog
lover in our family, and it wasn't long before I

1 The following lengthy story is adapted from my book *The
Beatles, God, and the Bible* (with kind permission from the
publisher, WND Books).

began using pictures of puppies to talk my wife, Sue, into getting another dog. Soon we located a litter of the cutest Bichon pups.

As we were looking at them, the owners asked if we wanted to meet the father of the litter. We said that we would. A door was opened and a fast-moving father ran around the room like a maniac then was quickly ushered into another room. We picked a pup, and as we were walking out the door, the owner commented, "Good luck." That seemed a little strange, but it was a statement that would come back to haunt us.

It wasn't long before Sam, the cutest little dog you have ever seen, was part of our family. It was a joy to once again hear the pitter-patter of little paws around the house. Knowing that Sue wasn't the type of person who would ever think of letting a dog lick her face (the sign of a true dog lover), I resolved to show my own appreciation for his place in our home by being quick to clean up after him.

Sam was the most wonderful-natured dog I have ever had. If he was chewing a bone and you got too close, he would stop eating, lick your hand, and then bring his bone closer to you so that you could be a guest at the table.

There was only one problem with him. He was an idiot. As he grew, he would run at you. Not to you. *At* you. If you were sitting on a couch, he would run across your shoulders, and even sit on your head. More than once, he ran at a portable table on which I had placed a full cup, and put his paws on the table. Each time, I would yell, "No!" at which point he would push away, sending the hot liquid flying.

Every night, for about two hours, he would go crazy—running around the house like a mad dog with the energy of a two-year-old on steroids, jumping on and off of Sue's lap, around her shoulders, down the hall, and back again. It was no exaggeration to say he was "bouncing off the walls." He used the couches to defy gravity as he bounded off of them. He chewed our furniture, gnawed windowsills, knocked pictures off the walls and chewed them, and ripped up any paper he could find.

He would go through the trash bin, open cupboard doors, and lift container lids to eat brownies (five at a time). He would wet the bed (not his—ours), burst out the front door onto the road if given half a chance, cry if he was left downstairs at night, whimper outside our bedroom door, drive visitors crazy, scratch, lick, whine, and he would even get on top of the kitchen table after a meal and sneakily eat any leftovers. I guess he learned this after he discovered how to climb up onto the kitchen counter and eat any food he could find. Worst of all, he would take food off my plate while it was still on my lap! If I disciplined him, that was obviously a game, which sent him into more tail-wagging excitement.

A game he loved was staring you down, but if he thought you were winning, he changed the game to "lunge at the nose." When he went to the groomers, they would graciously say he was "a handful." The vet called him "feisty." He once chewed the corner of my wallet, which he regularly emptied with vet fees. Often, Sue and I would lie awake at night and hear him get into the cupboard where we kept the pots and pans. I guess the cupboards reminded him of the chocolate cake he once ate in similar cupboards, which we had to secure with child-proof locks.

If I sat down to talk on the phone, he would get jealous and whine. If I tried to walk around during the conversation, he would wrap himself around my legs as I took a step. He did the same thing anytime I tried to walk downstairs. And he would throw himself against our bedroom door in the early hours of the morning and scare the living "nightlights" out of us.

I would continually tell Sue that it was just a matter of time until he matured. We could wait it out. Meanwhile, I diligently taught him to sit, lie down, jump, roll over, and shake hands. The only command he didn't obey was "Stay." And that was the one that mattered. It drove our stress levels off the charts. An elephant doing cartwheels each evening in the living room would have been less disruptive.

In an effort to keep the peace between Sue and Sam, I would make excuses for him: he's tired; he's young; he's still learning. But one evening, I was left excuseless. That was the time Sue was feeling really exhausted after a hard day. She dropped herself down on her favorite place to sit —our soft leather couch. Unfortunately, Sam had deposited Lake Superior on her seat. She sat in it and was coldly soaked to the skin. He had the whole house to use as a bathroom (not that he should have), and he chose that spot! I couldn't justify it. I should have known better. *Sam had to go.*

. . . .

I offered Sam as a gift to one friend who loved him. When he was seated, he would let Sam run all over him and even sit on his head. My friend, actor Kirk Cameron, who starred in the TV sitcom "Growing Pains" and movies like *Fireproof* and *Monumental*, said he would talk it over with his wife. A couple of days later, he graciously said she wanted a larger dog. I then offered Sam—plus five hundred dollars cash for dog food—to my buddy Mark Spence. Mark politely turned me down. I next offered him to another friend, Brad Snow, with a thousand dollars for dog food. He said he would give it some thought and talk it over with his wife. Soon, though, he respectfully rejected my offer. It looked like Sam was staying.

By his first birthday, believe it or not, there had been some real improvement. However, one day I was working in my garage/workshop when I heard a sound that's familiar to dog owners everywhere. This was about a month after Sam pulled the lid off the glue and ate half of the contents. Fortunately, it congealed and came back up as a rubber ball about the size of a small child's fist. This day, Sam was again making the now familiar "I'm getting ready to give dinner back to you" sound. I yelled, "No! Sam, *don't*. Go outside, now! Onto the lawn. *Now!* Go!" He didn't even look at me. He completely understood that I didn't want him throwing up in the garage, and quickly headed toward the door. He was being obedient, even in the middle of his suffering. How I love obedience. What a good dog. He ran through the garage door, turned a sharp left when he hit the lawn, charged up the steps, through the little doggy door, into the house—and threw up on our living room carpet!

But the worst came about a week after his first birthday. I had spent hours filming in Santa Monica in Southern California. It was even worth the three hours on the freeway to get there and back. I had one great interview that was good enough to make it onto the TV program I cohost. These are few and far between. Returning home, I left the MiniDV on my desk in my home office, planning to "log" it the next day. It *really* was a great interview.

When I arrived home that day, I found, to my horror, that Sam had chewed the cassette. I decided to try to save the tape, and put it into a new casing. After two to three hours of meticulous work, I finally did it. I slipped it into the camera to see if it would rewind, and it jammed the camera! I now had no tape, and it cost $250 to get it removed from the camera.

As time has passed, Sam has calmed down. Sort of. He still acts a little crazy now and then and sometimes plays a little dumb when I tell him to do things. But, like most dogs, if there is any meat in my hand he jumps through hoops for me faster than a hawk in a dive. Despite this small character weakness, he's a good dog. We hug, wrestle, chase cats together, have stare-downs, and really enjoy each other's company. He is forever trying to lick my face, and he's never so content as when he's sitting at my feet. When I get home in the evenings he almost breaks the door down he's so excited to see me. I have tried to train Sue to be like him. I can't tell you how much I love him. He inspired this book.

In the following pages, you will notice that all the annoying things dogs do are presented in the *male* gender. There are three reasons for this: 1) It would become tiresome to say "He or she…" 101 times. 2) The dog whose antics inspired this book is a male. And 3) I also wrote a book called *101 Things Husbands Do to Annoy Their Wives* (which Sue helped me write in ten minutes). That was in the male gender also…

1.

He whines at the door to get out.

Q. How do you keep a dog from
   barking in the front yard?
A. You place him in the back yard.

2.

He whines at the door to get in, two seconds
after whining to get out.

3.

He runs toward you playfully dropping a dog
biscuit at your feet, then picks it up and flings it
in the air giving the impression he wants to play.
When you get down on all fours to play,
he eats the biscuit.

4.

He scratches at the door until the paint
is worn away.

5.

He chews the nose off an expensive stuffed toy.

"Rambunctious, rumbustious, delinquent dogs
become angelic when sitting."
DR. IAN DUNBAR

6.

As you are waiting to close a door, he walks
through at a funeral pace.

7.

When you want to do something, he takes the
time to scratch first.

8.

He scratches at the door, then when you open it
to let him in, he looks at you with an expression
of "What do you want?"

9.

He pulls food out of his dish and places it on the clean floor to eat.

10.

He drinks so loudly the neighbors complain.

"Don't accept your dog's admiration as
conclusive evidence that you are wonderful."
ANN LANDERS

11.

He scratches the sofa in one spot, doing as much damage as possible.

12.

He barks at nothing.

13.

He barks in the night at every sound.

"I bought a dog the other day. I named him
Stay. It's fun to call him: 'Come here, Stay!
Come here, Stay!' He went insane."
STEVEN WRIGHT

14.

He scratches incessantly as though
he has 10,000 fleas.

15.

He jumps on and licks visitors
who don't like dogs.

16.

He licks himself, and then licks the baby's mouth.

"Things I learned from a dog:
If you don't have to go somewhere,
stay under the covers as long as possible."
UNKNOWN

17.

He throws up during the night, right where you walk in the morning.

18.

He goes to sleep in your favorite chair.

Q. Why do Dalmatians ride along
on fire trucks?
A. So they can help locate the fire hydrant.

19.

He growls when you come anywhere near the
food that *you* gave him.

20.

He gets under your feet—especially when you're
carrying something.

21.

He sheds his fur on everything.

"Outside of a dog, a book is probably
man's best friend, and inside of a dog,
it's too dark to read."
GROUCHO MARX

22.

Just when you're deep in thought, he barks really loud and scares the living daylights out of you.

23.

He chews in a way that makes a pig look like it has manners.

24.

He begs like he's starving for food. When you sacrifice your favorite delectable for him, he refuses to eat it.

25.

He knows how to do incredible tricks, but when you try to get him to do them in front of visitors, he acts like he's had his brain removed.

26.

He turns up his nose at expensive dog food.

"No matter how little money
and how few possessions you own,
having a dog makes you rich."
LOUIS SABIN, All About Dogs As Pets

27.

When you excitedly point at a cat on your fence,
he looks at your finger.

28.

He gets entangled in his leash.

Q. What dog will laugh at any joke?
A. A Chi-ha-ha.

29.

When you are leaning back in your recliner,
he lies down under the footrest.

30.

He hears the words "Stop that!" as an invitation to lick you once more.

31.

He walks in circles 68 times before lying down.

"A dog teaches a boy fidelity, perseverance,
and to turn around three times
before lying down."
ROBERT BENCHLEY

32.

He gets close enough to exhale
dog breath on you.

33.

He lies down right where people have to walk.

"A watchdog is a dog kept to guard your home,
usually by sleeping where a burglar would
awaken the household by falling over him."
UNKNOWN

34.

He chews any credit cards he finds.

*"Never judge a dog's pedigree by the
kind of books he does not chew."*
UNKNOWN

35.

He gets excited about going for a ride, then
whines at everything he sees.

36.

He puts his nose into dead flies, then licks them.

Q. How do you keep a dog from smelling?
A. You hold its nose.

37.

He brings the ball to you, then when you try to take it out of his mouth he turns his head away.

38.

He drops the ball for you out of arm's reach.

"I put contact lenses in my dog's eyes. They had little pictures of cats on them. Then I took one out and he ran around in circles."
STEVEN WRIGHT

39.

He gets food stuck to his facial fur.

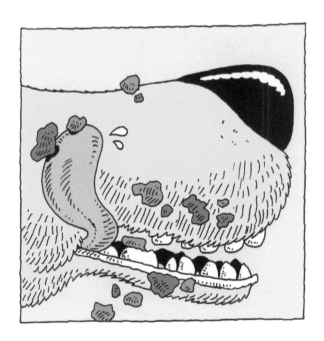

40.

He pushes his whole body weight on your legs.

Q. Why are Dalmatians no good at
"Hide and Seek"?
A. They're always spotted.

41.

He instigates playing with the ball,
then runs off with it.

42.

He sneezes on your foot.

*"You always sympathize with the underdog,
except when the other dog is yours."*
UNKNOWN

43.

He rolls in something dead and smelly.

44.

He eats your food when you're not looking.

"No man can be condemned for owning a dog.
As long as he has a dog, he has a friend; and
the poorer he gets, the better friend he has."
WILL ROGERS

45.

He jumps on you and scratches your bare arms.

46.

He stuffs himself with food then develops a look of "I haven't eaten for weeks..." during mealtime.

47.

His excessive drool puddles on the floor.

"*I think animal testing is a terrible idea; they get all nervous and give the wrong answers.*"
UNKNOWN

48.

He gets in the car and jumps back and forth over the seats like a maniac.

49.

He gets under your feet when you're driving.

"We derive immeasurable good, uncounted
pleasures, enormous security, and many
critical lessons about life by owning dogs."
ROGER CARAS, A Celebration of Dogs

50.

He jumps onto your lap when you're driving.

"Dogs feel very strongly that they should
always go with you in the car, in case the
need should arise for them to bark violently
at nothing right in your ear."
DAVE BARRY

51.

He knocks decorations off coffee tables with
his wagging tail.

52.

He walks in mud, then jumps
all over the furniture.

53.

He scrapes and rubs his dirty body
along the draperies.

"I spilled Spot Remover on my dog.
He's gone now."
STEVEN WRIGHT

54.

After drinking from his water bowl, he drips all over the floor as he walks away.

55.

He scratches one place until he wears
the fur away.

56.

When you point at something, he looks at everything else.

57.

He walks into spider webs.

"Whoever said you can't buy happiness
forgot about little puppies."
GENE HILL

58.

He shakes while he is being bathed.

"Even the tiniest poodle is lionhearted,
ready to do anything to defend home,
master, and mistress."
UNKNOWN

59.

After his bath, he soaks the room by shaking
all over everything.

60.

He avoids weeds and instead stomps on flowers.

"I am as confounded by dogs
as I am indebted to them."
ROGER CARAS, A Celebration of Dogs

61.

He treats all visitors as potential "ball throwers."

62.

Despite having a sense of smell 500 times
stronger than a human's, he sticks his nose
right into dirty things.

63.

He walks directly in front of the camera whenever a baby is being filmed or photographed.

64.

He never lets anyone open a bag of potato chips
without his being there within two seconds.

65.

He cultivates "my owner is choking me" noises
when he is on a leash.

66.

He slobbers on windows.

"There is no psychiatrist in the world like
a puppy licking your face."
BEN WILLIAMS

67.

He licks cushions.

68.

He wakes up well before dawn and scratches on your bedroom door.

69.

He acts like every guest has come to see him
and he's the center of attention.

70.

He forms tears in his eyes when someone
is eating.

*"If dogs could talk, it would take a lot of
the fun out of owning one."*
ANDY ROONEY

71.

He swallows food in big clumps, without chewing it, then makes loud choking noises.

72.

He wags his tail with enthusiasm while you are eating, like he believes you're about to share your food.

73.

He leaves partially chewed dog biscuits
around the house.

74.

He tilts his head to give a look of
"I can't believe you are eating that food
without giving me some!"

75.

He noses the ball so it rolls into your path.

"Did you ever notice when you blow in a dog's
face he gets mad at you? But when you take
him in a car he sticks his head out the window."
STEVE BLUESTONE

76.

He doesn't eat his food until you have eaten yours (you're no doubt eating something better).

77.

He coerces the baby to throw food over the edge of his high chair.

78.

If a pregnant woman is lying on the couch,
he jumps on her stomach.

79.

He puts his nose in your mouth when you yawn.

"Dogs come when they're called;
cats take a message and get back to you later."
MARY BLY

80.

He licks his belly until it's raw.

"I wonder if other dogs think poodles are members of a weird religious cult."
RITA RUDNER

81.

He snaps at flying insects.

82.

He puts his head in the way of food that is being put in the dog bowl.

83.

He puts his head in the way of water that is being poured into the dog bowl.

84.

He has an intense fascination with human morning breath.

85.

He barks at a prowling cat at 3:00 a.m.

"The average dog is a nicer person
than the average person."
ANDY ROONEY

86.

He chews on the remote control.

"A dog can express more with his tail in minutes than his owner can express with his tongue in hours."
UNKNOWN

87.

If a car alarm accidentally goes off, he adds to the confusion by howling.

88.

He sneezes 40 times in a row.

"Dogs are not our whole life,
but they make our lives whole."
ROGER CARAS, A Celebration of Dogs

89.

He walks around with flower petals or leaves
stuck to his nose.

90.

When the neighborhood dogs are howling,
he joins in the chorus.

91.

He acquires a breath similar to the smell at the bottom of a trashcan.

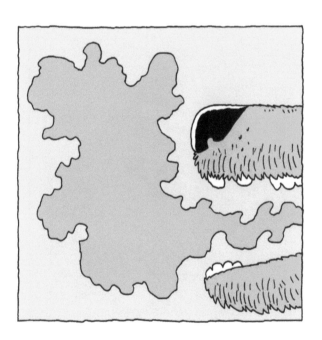

92.

He scratches his ears until the fur turns to dreadlocks.

93.

When it's bath time, he reacts like you're an enemy trying to drown him.

94.

He trembles with terror while being bathed.

95.

He digs holes in the garden.

"In order to keep a true perspective of one's importance, everyone should have a dog that will worship him and a cat that will ignore him."
DEREKE BRUCE

96

He overly sniffs visitors to a point of embarrassment.

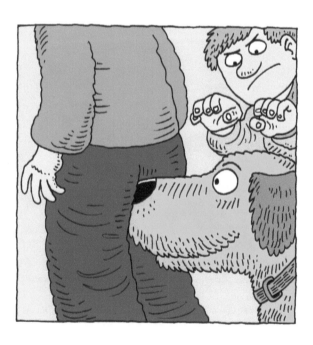

97.

He remembers how to do tricks, only in the face of a tasty treat.

98.

When pills are subtly hidden within a treat,
he eats the treat but spits out the pill.

99.

He jumps on freshly made beds.

"The difference between friends and pets is
that friends we allow into our company,
pets we allow into our solitude."
ROBERT BRAULT

100.

He barks during your Sunday afternoon nap.

"If you pick up a starving dog and make him prosperous, he will not bite you; that is the principal difference between a dog and a man."
MARK TWAIN

101.

He runs into a busy street to see if he can
cause an accident.

Appendix

I hope this book made you smile. That was one reason I wrote it. The other reason was to talk with you about life's most important issue.

I have often thought how much happier life would be if only my dog could understand English. I don't mean words like "sit" and "stay." I mean complete sentences like, "If you want to continually lick things, do it somewhere else. The slurping sound makes me feel sick. I love you, but when I'm snoozing, please don't bark loudly at nothing. It scares the living daylights out of me. Okay?" I would also tell him that we could both be millionaires if he would just say something like, "Boy, this dog food is really good!"

The reason I can't *reason* with my dog is that he's from a different "kind." He has many of the same features that people have—eyes, ears, nose, mouth, heart, lungs, liver, etc., as do many of the other animals—but human beings are unique in creation. We are aware of our "being." Each of us has the knowledge that we are going to die. We have thoughts about life's purpose and where we will spend eternity. Something within the heart of every sane human being says, "Oh, I don't want to die!" So here is perhaps the most profound of life's great questions: where will you go when you die? Have you figured that one out yet? Do you think you will go to Heaven because you are a good person? Years ago, if you asked me if I was a good person, I would have answered that I was. I would have said, "If there is a Heaven, I will probably make it because I'm not a bad person." But I was making a terrible mistake. God has a list of ten things we must do—they are called the Ten Commandments. In my ignorance, I didn't realize that I had already broken those Commandments and was in great danger.

The biblical explanation about why each of us will die is that we have broken an uncompromising law. Just as we suffer the consequences if we step off a ten-story building, so we will suffer the consequences of transgressing God's Moral Law. Let's see if you have broken the Ten Commandments: 1) Is God first in your life? Do you love Him with all of your heart, soul, mind, and strength? Do you love your neighbor as yourself? Does your love for your family seem like hatred, compared to the love you have for the One who

. . . .

gave those loved ones to you? 2) Have you made a god in your own image, to suit yourself—a god you are more comfortable with? 3) Have you ever used God's holy name in vain—substituting it for a four-lettered filth word to express disgust, or using it as a "meaningless" expression like "Oh my god"? 4) Have you kept the Sabbath holy? 5) Have you always honored your parents? 6) Have you hated anyone? Then the Bible says you are a murderer. 7) Have you had sex before marriage? Or have you lusted after another person? The Bible warns that you have committed adultery in your heart. 8) Have you ever stolen anything? Then you are a thief. 9) If you have told even one lie, you are a liar, and cannot enter the Kingdom of God. 10) Finally, have you ever jealously desired something that belonged to someone else? Then you have broken the Tenth Commandment.

Listen to your conscience. The Law leaves us all sinners in God's sight. On Judgment Day we will be found guilty, and will end up in Hell forever. Perhaps you are sorry for your sins, and you even confess them to God. But that doesn't mean He will forgive you, regardless of how sincere you are. Let me explain why. Imagine you are standing guilty in front of a judge, facing a $50,000 fine, and say, "Judge, I'm truly sorry for my crime." He would probably say, "So you should be! Now are you able to pay the $50,000 fine or not?" A judge must have grounds upon which he can release you. If someone paid your fine, only then would you be free from the demands of the law.

That's precisely what God did in the person of Jesus Christ. Each of us stands guilty of breaking God's Law, but because Jesus paid our fine on the cross 2,000 years ago, God can forgive us on the grounds of His suffering death. That's why you need Jesus Christ as your Savior. Without Him, the Law will send you to Hell, and you will have no one to blame but yourself. God will make sure justice is carried out.

The Bible says, "God demonstrates His own love toward us, in that while we were still sinners, Christ died for us" (Romans 5:8). Jesus, the Son of God, gave His sinless life on the cross, showing the depth of God's love for us. We broke God's Law, and He paid our fine so that we could be free from its perfect demands. Then He rose from the dead, and defeated the power of the grave. The Bible says that all humanity is held captive to the fear of death (Hebrews 2:15). If you don't face your fear of death, then you will run from it until

. . . .

the day you die…and that day *will* come. The proof of your sinfulness will be your death. Today, not only face the reality that you will die, *but do something about it:* obey the gospel and live. If you repent (turn from your sins) and place your trust in the Savior, God will forgive your sins and grant you everlasting life.

I try to be diligent when it comes to teaching my dog obedience. There is a very good reason for this. When I was 18 years old I had a fun-loving Corgi named Jordy. We lived about a hundred yards from the beach, and I would take him along when I went surfing and he would spend his time chasing seagulls until I came in from the waves. He loved our times together, and if I as much as mumbled the word "beach," he would run around in circles of excitement.

Around 4 p.m. one Saturday, I said we are going to the beach and Jordy did his usual circles of joy from the time we left home. As we walked along the sidewalk, suddenly he ran ahead of me. I called for him to come back, but he was so excited he didn't obey me. I called him again and again,

...and as he dashed across the road he was hit by a car.

I will never forget seeing his body (in what seemed like slow motion) go under the car, and then get shot out the back. I dropped my brand new surfboard on the sidewalk and ran into the road, picked up my beloved dog, ran home, and sat on the driveway cradling him in my arms. As I looked down at him I saw a hole on the top of his head and blood dripping out of his mouth. I then looked up and saw that the car that hit him had parked opposite where I sat. The driver got out, walked over to me, put his hand on my shoulder and burst into tears.

The next day the veterinarian told us that Jordy's injuries were so extensive they had to put him to sleep.

That night I thought seriously about God and the issues of life and death for the first time. I also thought about Jordy's lack of obedience, and oh how I wished he had come back when I called his name.

God wants to keep us away from that which will kill us. That's why He commands us to turn around through repentance, and wonder of wonders, upon conversion we receive a new heart

· ·

that longs to be obedient to His voice. When we are born again we have a new nature that says, "I delight to do your will, oh my God."

Please, confess your sins to God, put your faith in Jesus Christ, then read the Bible daily and obey what you read. God will never let you down.

Thanks for reading this. Feel free to go to LivingWaters.com and click on "Save Yourself Some Pain."

This book is available in bulk at a very low cost. Please, consider purchasing copies and giving them away. For other books, videos, etc., by Ray Comfort, visit LivingWaters.com or call 800-437-1893.